FEAR

THE SILENT ENEMY

CLARENCE KD MCNAIR

ISBN-13: 978-1-954609-87-7

Library of Congress Control Number: 2025920027

This book was printed in the United States of America

For information regarding special discounts for bulk purchases, please contact the publisher:

LaBoo Publishing Enterprise, LLC
staff@laboopublishing.com
www.laboopublishing.com

Connect with the author on all social media @clarencekdmcnair

ENDORSEMENT

Clarence McNair has written a timely, powerful, and necessary declaration of war against fear. In a world consumed by anxiety, uncertainty, and control, this book is a bold reminder that fear is not from God—and we don't have to live under its rule.

Clarence doesn't just talk about fear; he confronts it head-on, exposing the societal lies and spiritual strongholds that have kept so many bound. As I read through these pages, I saw a warrior rising—one who understands that fear is a spirit and must be fought spiritually. Clarence equips readers with faith-based principles, prayer strategies, and biblical truths that mirror the very heartbeat of what I teach in *Ferocious Warrior*. His message is raw, honest, and anointed.

This book is more than encouragement—it's activation. If you're ready to silence the voice of fear and walk boldly into your God-given purpose, Clarence McNair is the voice you need.

—Cora Jakes
Author of *Ferocious Warrior*
Faith leader, mentor, and warrior for the broken

Fear can only survive
on the residue of your
insecurities.

Dice Gamble

DEDICATION

For Dereck Green —

My good friend, my brother in spirit,

whose presence brought light, laughter, and strength.

Though you're no longer here in body,

your legacy, love, and inspiration live on in these pages.

This book is for you.

TABLE OF CONTENTS

FOREWORD
By Cora Jakes

Fear is a liar.

It's persistent, persuasive, and patient—waiting for the right moment to slip into your thoughts and convince you that you are powerless, inadequate, and unworthy. But the most dangerous thing about fear isn't just what it says, it's how quietly and subtly it controls. In today's society, fear has become a tool of manipulation. It's broadcast through news headlines, embedded in social media, reinforced in culture, and disguised as wisdom. Fear has become a system—designed to hold people back from walking in the fullness of who God created them to be.

But thank God for truth-tellers and faith-warriors like Clarence McNair—bold enough to confront fear head-on and equip others to do the same.

When Clarence told me about this book, I knew it would be more than just another motivational read. This book is a weapon. A spiritual blueprint. A call to arms for anyone who has ever been imprisoned by fear and is ready to break free.

As someone who has walked through deep pain, spiritual warfare, and countless seasons of fear-based attacks, I understand the weight fear can carry. I also understand the authority we have as believers to crush it. And that's exactly what Clarence teaches in this book—not how to manage fear, but how to conquer it.

2 Timothy 1:7 declares, "For God has not given us a spirit of fear, but of power, love, and a sound mind." That scripture is more than a comfort, it's a compass. If fear didn't come from God, it has no legal right to govern your decisions, define your identity, or dictate your future. What God gave you is power. Love. A sound mind. These are spiritual tools for spiritual battles. This is what we fight with.

Clarence gets it. He digs into the truth that fear is not just emotional, it is spiritual. And to defeat it, you must be spiritually equipped. The world teaches us to rely on logic and self-help. But when the fear you're facing is fueled by systems and spirits, you need more than affirmations. You need the Word of God. You need prayer. Discernment. You need the Holy Spirit.

In my book *Ferocious Warrior*, I wrote, "If you want to defeat the enemy, you have to change the way you fight."

Clarence embodies that principle in this book. He doesn't just expose fear—he teaches you how to dismantle it. He reveals how society strategically uses fear is used through media, money, politics, and even religion to shape behavior and suppress truth. But you were never meant to live in fear. You were born to live in faith.

This book also reminds me of another key principle from *Ferocious Warrior*. "A prayerless warrior is a powerless warrior." And let me tell you something—Clarence is not a powerless man. He has learned how to war in the Spirit. To pray through pain. To fight through fear. And now he's teaching you to do the same.

One of the most transformative truths in this book is the idea that you have authority over fear. That doesn't mean fear won't show up. It means fear won't win. Clarence gives practical and spiritual steps to help you see how fear operates in your life and how to shut it down—whether it's fear of failure, rejection, lack, or stepping into your calling. This book walks you through how to evict fear from your mind, your spirit, and your future.

Isaiah 41:10 says, "So do not fear, for I am with you; do not be dismayed, for I am your God. I will strengthen you and help you; I will uphold you with my righteous right hand."

That verse is your divine reminder that you are never alone in your fight. God is your strength, your support, and your safe place. When fear screams, His love speaks louder. When anxiety rises, His peace calms the storm.

This book isn't just encouragement—it's empowerment. Clarence doesn't just speak to your ears; he speaks to your spirit. He reminds you that you are not weak. You are not fragile. You are not a victim of fear. You are a ferocious warrior—and this is your war cry.

So before you turn the page and dive into Clarence's powerful insights, I want to cover you in prayer. Not a gentle prayer—but a warfare prayer. Because if you're going to conquer fear, you'll have to pray like you've never prayed before.

A PRAYER TO CONQUER FEAR

Heavenly Father,

We come before You today with boldness, standing in the full authority You have given us as sons and daughters of the Kingdom. Today, we declare that fear no longer has a home in our minds, our hearts, or our future.

We break every agreement we've made with fear—spoken or unspoken, known or unknown. We come out of covenant with every lie that says we're not enough, that we'll fail, that we'll never be free. We renounce every word curse, every generational fear, every trauma-based fear, and every system that has used fear to manipulate us.

In Psalm 27:1, Your Word says, "The Lord is my light and my salvation—whom shall I fear?" Father, we declare that we will fear no one and nothing but You. We trust You as our Defender, our Redeemer, our Protector, and our Provider.

We put on the full armor of God—belt of truth, breastplate of righteousness, shoes of peace, shield of faith, helmet of salvation, and the sword of the Spirit. We use these weapons to fight every spiritual force of fear that has tried to keep us bound.

God, give us holy boldness. Give us clarity in confusion. Give us peace in chaos. Teach us to war in the spirit. Teach us to fast strategically. Teach us to worship deeply, declare prophetically, and pray ferociously.

We will not bow to fear.

We will not be silenced.

We will not shrink back.

We are warriors. We are free. We are fierce. We are faithful.

And we are walking forward—without fear. In Jesus' mighty, matchless name, it is so, and so it is. Amen.

To Clarence—I honor your obedience, your bravery, and your heart for God's people. Thank you for turning your own battles into a roadmap for others. You have birthed something powerful.

To the reader—this book is a key. Use it. Let it unlock your courage, your voice, and your destiny. Don't just read it. War with it.

Now go.

Be bold.

Be fearless.

Be ferocious.

~ Cora Jakes

INTRODUCTION

For many of us, fear is the number one enemy. It's the invisible force that controls thoughts, dictates our actions, and keeps our dreams locked away. Fear distorts reality, it makes problems feel bigger than they are and obstacles seem insurmountable. It whispers doubts in your ear. *You're not good enough. You'll fail, Don't even try.*

Because of fear, countless people have missed out on opportunities—jobs they never applied for, relationships they never pursued, ideas they never shared. Some stay stuck in the same routine, afraid to step outside of their comfort zone because the unknown feels too risky. Others are paralyzed by fear of failure or rejection, caught in a cycle of self-doubt and hesitation.

But what if you could break free?

This book is about facing your fears, understanding them, and learning how to use them—not as a roadblock, but as a catalyst for growth. Fear doesn't have to be the enemy. It can be the very thing that pushes you to rise above limitations and step fully into your potential.

In the pages ahead, you'll discover:

- Why fear has such a strong hold on you—and how it shapes your decisions.

- How to reframe fear as fuel instead of something that stops you.

- Practical strategies to face and overcome fear in different areas of life.

- The mindset shifts that will unlock confidence, courage, and success.

At one point, fear showed up in my life—but I made it clear: *You can't live here.*

ONE

RECOGNIZING FEAR – THE SILENT FORCE HOLDING YOU BACK

Many people don't realize they're living in fear. It doesn't always show up as panic or anxiety—sometimes, it's much quieter. Fear can look like playing it safe, sticking to routines, avoiding discomfort, or convincing yourself that you're "just being realistic." It can feel like hesitation, doubt, or an invisible force keeping you from taking action.

Fear doesn't always come with a racing heart or shaky hands. Sometimes it shows up in more subtle ways:

- **Procrastination** – You keep putting off your goals, telling yourself you'll start "when the time is right."

- **Perfectionism** – You tell yourself you need to be fully prepared before taking action, but deep down, you're just afraid of failing.

- **Overthinking** – You analyze every decision until you feel stuck, afraid of making the wrong move.

- **Excuses** – "I'm too busy." "It's not the right time." "I don't have enough experience." These might sound logical, but they often cover up fear.

- **Seeking Validation** – You look for reassurance from others instead of trusting your own instincts.

- **Staying in Your Comfort Zone** – You tell yourself you're happy where you are, but deep down, you feel stuck or unfulfilled.

Solution: Reclaim Your Own Standards

- Identify whose expectations you're living by – Write down the beliefs or pressures you feel. Are they truly yours, or were they passed on to you by others—family, or culture, or society?

- Redefine success on your terms – Focus on what makes *you* truly happy rather than external validation to internal fulfillment. What truly makes you happy?

- Set boundaries – Learn to say no to expectations that don't align with your values.

- Affirm your right to choose – Remind yourself daily: *"I am free to live life on my own terms."*

TWO
THE COST OF LIVING IN FEAR

When fear controls your life, you don't just avoid danger, you avoid growth. You stay in the same job even though you dream of something more. You hold back from expressing your true thoughts because you're worried about judgment. You let opportunities pass because stepping into the unknown feels too risky.

But here's the truth: Fear doesn't keep you safe, it keeps you *small*.

The first step to overcoming fear is recognizing it. It's time to ask yourself:

- Where am I holding myself back?

- What dreams have I ignored because they seemed too scary?

- Am I making choices based on what I truly want— or what I'm afraid of?

This book will help you uncover these hidden fears and give you the tools to move past them. Because once you recognize fear for what it is, you take away its power.

Are you ready to take control?

Living in a World of Fear

For some, fear isn't just an occasional emotion—it becomes a way of life. Many people live in a constant state of anxiety and shape their decisions, relationships, and ambitions around fear instead of possibility. Rather than embracing opportunities, they remain trapped in a cycle of worry, not realizing how much they're holding themselves back. This mindset doesn't develop overnight. It's often a result of conditioning—where fear gradually takes over and becomes the default way of living.

A major contributor to this fear-based mindset is the media we consume. News, television, and social media bombard us with negativity—disasters, crime, economic collapse, and sensationalized tragedies. These platforms thrive on fear because fear grabs attention. And the more we're exposed to those messages, the more our minds are programmed to see the world as dangerous and unpredictable, making us hesitant to step outside our comfort zones. Instead of being a tool for learning and growth, the media becomes a source of anxiety that limits our perspectives.

Another big factor in a fear-driven life is the people we surround ourselves with. People who are scared tend to project their insecurities and fears onto others, discouraging risk-taking and the pursuit of dreams. I call these people *"fear-trippers."*

THREE

THE LOST INNOCENCE - HOW FEAR REPLACES FREEDOM

When a child is born, they come into this world in a state of pure peace. They don't know fear, stress, or responsibility. Their eyes are wide with wonder, and their hearts are free to experience joy without hesitation. At birth, there are no burdens weighing them down—only curiosity, trust, and an unshaken belief in the safety of the world around them. But as they grow, something begins to change.

The world slowly introduces them to its expectations, pressures, and fears. Some of this is natural—learning about danger helps us survive—but much of it is unnecessary. Many children are burdened with responsibilities beyond their years, their innocence stripped away too soon by the stress and worry of the adults around them.

11

The Weight of Adult Worries

Too often, parents and caregivers unknowingly project their own fears onto their children. A mother constantly worried about money may raise a child who fears scarcity. A father who always warns about failure may instill a fear of making mistakes. The home—meant to be a place of safety and encouragement—can become the very place where a child first learns to doubt themselves and the world.

Some children grow up never truly feeling safe. They live on edge, absorbing their caregivers' anxieties. Instead of exploring life with curiosity, they move through it cautiously, afraid to step out of line, afraid of disappointing others, afraid of the unknown. This fear, once planted, takes root and shapes the way they see the world for years.

The Foundation That Shapes a Life

A child's early experiences create the foundation for their future. If that foundation is built on fear, stress, and uncertainty, they may grow into adults who struggle with confidence, decision-making, and peace of mind. But when the foundation is built on love, safety, and support, children grow up with the tools they need to face life's challenges with resilience and courage.

What if we prioritized protecting a child's innocence for as long as possible? What if we let them believe in possibility before introducing them to limits? What if we taught them that they are safe, capable, and worthy—instead of burdening them with grown-up worries too soon?

Breaking the Cycle

Many adults today live with fears instilled in their childhood. They were taught to fear failure, rejection, or simply not being enough. Those fears dictate their choices, keeping them stuck in jobs they hate, relationships that drain them, and lives that feel unfulfilled.

But here's the truth—fear is learned. And that means it can be unlearned. The first step is figuring out where it started. Most of the fear we carry isn't even ours. It was passed down by well-meaning but fearful adults. Understanding this is the first step toward letting go.

We can also break this cycle for the next generation. Instead of fear, we can pass down confidence. Instead of caution, we can teach courage. By allowing children to hold onto their innocence longer, we give them a stronger foundation—one built on self-trust, optimism, and freedom.

Reclaiming Innocence as Adults

We can't go back and relive childhood—but we can reconnect with the parts of ourselves that were lost along the way. Who were you before fear entered your life? What did you believe about the world before you were taught to be afraid?

Overcoming fear begins with reclaiming that childlike wonder—the part of you that still believes that anything is possible. It's not about ignoring reality. It's about changing how you see it. Life doesn't have to be lived in fear. And safety doesn't always come from control. True security comes from trust—trust in yourself, in your ability to handle challenges, and in the idea that not everything is meant to be feared.

By preserving innocence in children and reclaiming it as adults, we create a world where fear no longer dictates our lives. We move forward with courage—and give the next generation permission to do the same.

FOUR
EMBRACING THE UNKNOWN

Fear of the unknown is one of the greatest barriers to personal freedom. We convince ourselves that staying in the familiar—even when it limits us—is safer than stepping into uncertainty. We hesitate, overthink, and talk ourselves out of opportunities simply because we don't know what's on the other side. But life itself is unpredictable—every moment, every breath, every step is a walk into the unknown. The more we resist that truth, the more we trap ourselves in a cycle of fear and hesitation.

We often call our hesitation "protecting ourselves," but more often than not, it's just fear in disguise. We stay in relationships that no longer serve us, jobs that leave us feeling empty, and routines that keep us stagnant, all because they're familiar. The unknown feels like a threat, when really, it's where growth and transformation live. Every breakthrough, every moment of expansion, comes from stepping beyond the boundaries of what we know.

Think about the most meaningful moments in your life, none of them came from standing still. That change, that relationship, that success—they happened because you leaped into something uncertain. The fear you felt didn't stop the outcome; it was just an illusion keeping you in place. If we accept that uncertainty is a constant, we can stop fighting it and start flowing with it.

We were never meant to control everything. The idea that we can predict or manipulate life to fit our expectations is an illusion. What if, instead of fearing uncertainty, we got excited about it? Imagine waking up knowing that something new could happen—something to discover, experience, and help you grow.

Releasing fear of the unknown doesn't mean diving into situations recklessly. It means trusting that you have the strength, wisdom, and resilience to handle whatever comes. You don't need to know every step before you start walking. You just need the courage to take the first one, trusting that the path will reveal itself as you go.

Life isn't about waiting for certainty—it's about dancing with uncertainty. The greatest joys, the most profound love, and the deepest experiences come when we stop clinging to what we know and start exploring what we don't. Every day is an invitation to step into something new. To take a risk. To allow the unknown to shape us in ways we never imagined.

So if everything is unknown anyway, why not embrace it? Why not trust that no matter what happens, you will find your way? The unknown is not your enemy—it is your greatest adventure. And the sooner you release your fear of it, the sooner you'll truly start living.

The Solution: Stay True to Yourself

First, you have to understand this: *You are enough just being you.*

Your worth isn't based on your job, success, relationships, or what people think about you.

Here's what you can start doing:

1. **Spend Time Getting to Know Yourself Again**

   Figure out who you are without the titles, money, relationships, or fame.

   Ask yourself:

   - What makes me happy?
   - What makes me laugh?
   - What do I love doing even if no one claps for me?

Write it down if you need to. You've got to know who you are when the lights are off and no one's watching.

2. Practice Saying "No"

You don't have to say yes to everything and everyone.

Saying no protects your peace.

If something feels wrong, it's okay to say no—even if people don't like it.

Remember: if saying yes hurts you, it's the wrong yes.

3. Stop Chasing Approval

You don't need everyone to like you.

Even if the whole world claps for you, it won't matter if you don't clap for yourself.

Start asking:

- Do I like me?
- Am I proud of who I am?

Your opinion of yourself matters more than anyone else's.

4. Learn to Let Go

If people walk away because you're being your true self, let them go.

The right people will love you for who you really are.

Don't hold onto people who only like the "performance" version of you.

5. Stay Connected to What You Love

Don't let success or failure change your heart.

Keep doing the things you love—even if no one's watching, even if no one's paying you.

That's how you stay grounded and close to your real self.

6. Be Patient with Yourself

Healing takes time. Growth takes time.

You will slip up. You'll have days where you feel lost again. That's okay.

Just don't give up.

Keep choosing yourself, every day.

In simple words:

You don't have to perform.

You don't have to shrink.

You don't have to fake it.

You just have to be real.

And protect that reality like your life depends on it—because it does.

FIVE

WASH YOUR FACE AND MOVE FORWARD

Our outer world is often a reflection of our inner world. How we see ourselves inside shapes how we show up in life. But too often, we get stuck in past experiences—mistakes, failures, heartbreaks, or traumas—that define our identity. Instead of moving forward, we live in the shadow of what once was. We allow the past to dictate our present and future. It's as if we're looking in a mirror that reflects only old wounds rather than the potential of who we can become.

But here's the truth—we have the power to cleanse ourselves of yesterday's burdens, to wash our face and step into a new version of ourselves.

One of the biggest reasons people stay trapped in the past is identity. If a painful experience shaped the way you see yourself, it can feel impossible to break free. A person who was betrayed may believe they can never trust again. Someone who failed at a dream might see themselves as someone who will never succeed. These beliefs become a cage. They stop us from taking risks, growing, or believing in possibilities. When your identity is tied to past pain, you unknowingly invite fear, doubt, and hesitation into your life.

But you are not your past. You are not the mistakes you made, the hurt you experienced, or the moments that broke you.

Fear thrives in uncertainty—especially when we feel like we don't have control over what happens next.

"What if this happens again?"

"What if I get hurt?"

"What if I fail?"

These questions keep us stuck because they focus on what we can't control instead of what we can.

But fear loses its power when we shift our focus.

Instead of asking, "What if I fail again?" ask, "What if I succeed?"

Instead of wondering, "What if I get hurt?" ask, "What if I heal and grow stronger?"

Moving forward starts with a change in your perspective. It's about being willing to believe that the future holds more than just a repeat of the past.

Healing doesn't mean forgetting—it means loosening the grip those experiences have on your life. It means recognizing that while the past shaped you, it doesn't have to define you.

Moving forward requires action—whether it's seeking help, changing your environment, or simply deciding to think differently.

Sometimes, it's as simple as washing your face—both literally and metaphorically. Cleanse yourself of the old stories, the self-doubt, the fear. Look in the mirror and see not who you were, but who you're becoming.

Life is about forward movement. Holding on to the past slows you down and keeps you from becoming the person you were meant to be.

Every single day is another chance to rewrite your story, take control of your narrative, and walk in the direction of growth and healing.

Don't let past pain be the weight that holds you back.

Wash your face.

Lift your head.

Move forward.

The life you want is waiting.

SIX
PROTECTING YOUR MIND AND ENERGY

One of the most important lessons in personal growth is understanding the power of your mindset. A growth mindset allows you to see challenges as opportunities, while a fixed mindset keeps you stuck in fear and self-doubt. The way you think influences your actions, and your actions shape your reality. If you want to grow, you must intentionally develop a mindset that encourages progress, resilience, and confidence. This means feeding your mind with positive influences, learning from failures, and continuously pushing yourself beyond your comfort zone.

Just as important is the company you keep. The people around you can either lift you up or tear you down. Who you allow in your life impacts your mindset. Some people inspire and support your growth. Others drain your energy, plant seeds of doubt, and hold you back from achieving your goals. You have to know the difference—and then make a conscious decision to surround yourself with those who uplift you. Protecting your mental and emotional space isn't selfish. It's necessary.

Letting go of toxic relationships can be difficult, especially if these individuals have been in your life for a long time. But you don't owe anyone access to your mind or energy if they're not contributing to your growth. Growth usually involves discomfort. And when you distance yourself from negativity, you create space for healthier connections that align with your goals and values. Your peace of mind and personal growth should always take precedence over maintaining relationships that hinder your potential.

But building a supportive environment isn't just about cutting off negativity. It's also about seeking out those who challenge and inspire you. Surround yourself with people who push you to grow, celebrate your successes, and keep you accountable to your goals. Have conversations that stimulate your mind. Read books. Listen to podcasts. Learn from those who have walked the path of success before you. The more you invest in personal development, the stronger your mindset will become.

Ultimately, protecting your mind means taking control of your life. You have the power to decide what influences you. You choose what to let in and what mindset you want to cultivate. Fear and negativity will always be present, but you don't have to let them define you. Focus on growth. Distance yourself from things that hold you back. Be intentional about the thoughts you entertain. When you commit to a growth mindset and protect your mental space, you set yourself up for a future of unlimited possibilities.

Guarding Your Greatest Asset

Your mind is your greatest asset. It's the foundation for all success, growth, and resilience. Like anything valuable, it must be protected. If you don't guard your mind, external influences—fear, doubt, and negativity—can take root and cloud your thinking. Your thoughts shape your reality, and the quality of your life is directly tied to the quality of your mind. That's why it's so important to become intentional about what enters and exits. Just like you wouldn't leave your front door open to intruders, you shouldn't leave your mind wide open to things that could weaken your confidence or distort your vision.

Monitoring what comes in and out of your mind is a daily discipline. Every conversation you have, every piece of media you take in, and every thought you let linger has the power to shape how you see yourself and the world. The more you entertain negativity, the more it settles in, keeping you stuck in a cycle. But when you actively filter your thoughts, focusing on what strengthens and uplifts you, you start to take control of your mental space. That doesn't mean ignoring reality or pretending challenges don't exist, it just means not letting destructive thoughts dictate your actions or limit your potential.

Beyond guarding your mind against external threats, you have to prepare it for the challenges that life will inevitably bring. Fear doesn't always come from the situation itself—it comes from being unprepared to handle the unknown. If you train your mind to remain flexible and forward focused, you won't get stuck in painful experiences or setbacks. Instead, you'll see obstacles as temporary, lessons as opportunities, and fear as something to move through—not something that holds you back. Preparation isn't just knowing what might happen, it's about training yourself to respond with resilience.

One of the biggest threats to your growth is allowing your mind to become trapped in a single moment, especially those involving pain, failure, or fear. When you replay the past over and over, you keep yourself locked in an experience that's already over. And that stops you from fully engaging in the present. Growth requires movement. And movement means letting go of anything that's chaining you to what was. The past has value only when it becomes a teacher—not as a prison. Learn the lesson. Then move forward.

The key to mastering your mind is discipline. This means being conscious of your thoughts, questioning limiting beliefs, and challenging fear when it arises. It takes daily effort—just like building a strong body through consistent training. You need routines that reinforce a powerful mindset—reading, journaling, practicing gratitude, and surrounding yourself with people who uplift you. The more disciplined you become in managing your mind, the less control external circumstances will have over you. You are no longer reactive but proactive. No longer a victim of your thoughts but the master of them.

Your mind determines the direction of your life, so guard it fiercely. Protect it from negative influences, train it for unexpected challenges, and refuse to let it dwell in places that hinder growth. When you take full responsibility for your mental state, you unlock the ability to navigate life with confidence and clarity. Fear may still show up, but it will no longer have the power to control you. Instead, you will face it head-on, knowing that you are equipped to overcome anything that stands in your way.

Fear isn't something we're born with—it's something we're taught. The great Creator made it clear: "For I did not give you the spirit of fear." That means fear isn't our natural state. It's learned. It's placed upon us by life experiences, circumstances, and even the people around us. From an early age, we begin absorbing fear—whether from warnings meant to protect us, painful experiences, or limitations imposed by others. That fear shapes how we see the world and how we see ourselves.

Life has a way of introducing fear at unexpected moments, sometimes as early as childhood. A child who is constantly told to be careful may grow up believing the world is dangerous. Someone who experiences loss at a young age may carry a fear of abandonment for the rest of their life. These early experiences lay the groundwork for how we handle fear later on. They shape our decisions, our relationships, and our ambitions. Over time, those fears become deeply rooted, making it difficult to tell what is real and what's just past pain replaying itself.

Fear tells us we're not good enough, not strong enough, and that failure is inevitable. It can stop people from chasing their dreams, taking risks, and becoming the person they're meant to be. The longer fear is allowed to take root, the more it grows—wrapping itself around every decision and trapping a person in their comfort zone.

But the Creator never intended for us to live this way.

Overcoming fear begins with recognizing that it's not part of our true nature. We were created to be bold, courageous, and full of purpose. When we understand that fear is something given to us—not something we're born with—we gain the power to reject it. We can trade fear for faith, uncertainty for confidence, and hesitation for action. The journey to overcoming fear isn't always easy, but it's necessary for true growth and freedom.

In the end, fear has only as much power as we give it. When we stop accepting it as part of our identity, we take the first step toward living a life of strength and purpose.

The Creator didn't give us the spirit of fear but of power, love, and a sound mind. If we hold onto that truth, we can break free from the chains of fear and step into the life we're meant to live.

SEVEN
THE POWER OF THOUGHT

Freedom begins in the mind. The thoughts we entertain shape our reality—they influence our decisions, emotions, and overall well-being. If we allow negativity, doubt, or fear to take root, they will control us, keeping us trapped in cycles of frustration and stagnation. Setting yourself free requires intentional thought management, choosing what you allow into your mental space and what you reject. Learning to filter your thoughts with clarity and purpose is the first step toward true freedom.

One of the most valuable skills you can develop is the ability to pause and think things through. Impulse decisions often lead to regret, while careful consideration paves the way to success and peace of mind. Instead of rushing in, take a step back. Grab a pen and pad and write it down. Whether it's a business venture, a new relationship, or a major life change, putting your thoughts on paper allows you to see them from a different perspective. Writing forces clarity—and clarity helps you decide if something aligns with your goals and values.

Boundaries protect your peace and progress. Without clear personal limits, you open yourself to being drained, misled, or taken advantage of. It's easy to say "yes" out of obligation, fear, or excitement—but every "yes" comes with a cost. The key is knowing what you're willing to accept and what you're not. This isn't about being rigid or closed off—it's about having the self-awareness to protect yourself from unnecessary stress and distractions. Standing firm in your boundaries is an act of self-respect.

Opportunities are everywhere, but not all of them are meant for you. Just because something looks good on the surface doesn't mean it's aligned with your path. The ability to discern what serves you and what doesn't is crucial. Every opportunity should be evaluated through the lens of your long-term vision.

- Will this help you grow?
- Will it bring you peace?
- Does it align with your purpose?

If the answer is no, then walking away isn't fear—it's wisdom.

The same goes for relationships. The people you surround yourself with shape your mindset and direction. Toxic relationships—whether personal or professional—can derail your progress, cloud your judgment, and drain your energy. You have to recognize when a relationship is serving you and when it's holding you back. Letting go of the wrong people makes room for the right ones.

Self-protection is your responsibility. No one else will guard your time, energy, and dreams the way you will. The more intentional you are about what you allow into your life, the more control you have over your future. This doesn't mean living in fear or being overly cautious. It's about being mindful, strategic, and in alignment with your purpose. Trust yourself to make decisions that serve your highest good.

At the end of the day, true freedom is about ownership. It's about owning your thoughts, choices, and direction. You get to decide what's on your plate—and you get to say "no" when it doesn't serve you. By thinking things through, setting boundaries, and protecting your peace, you create a life that is not just free but fulfilling. The journey to freedom starts with you.

EIGHT

OVERCOMING FEAR IN DIFFERENT AREAS OF LIFE USING 2 TIMOTHY 1:7

For God has not given us a spirit of fear,
but of power and of love and of a sound mind.

The truth in this verse applies to so many areas of life where fear tries to hold us back. Let's break down how we can use God's gifts—power, love, and a sound mind—to overcome fear in specific situations.

1. Fear of Failure (Career, Business, Goals)

Fear says: "What if I fail? What if I'm not good enough?"

God says: "I have given you power to succeed."

- **Power:** God has equipped you with talents, wisdom, and resilience. Failure isn't a final destination—it's a steppingstone to growth. Philippians 1:6 reminds us that "He who began a good work in you will carry it on to completion."

- **Love:** When you operate from love rather than fear, you pursue your purpose with passion rather than doubt.

- **Sound Mind:** Instead of dwelling on what could go wrong, think logically and strategically, and trust God to guide you. Proverbs 3:5-6 says to lean on Him for direction.

Application

- Take action despite fear. Confidence grows with experience.

- See setbacks as learning opportunities, not proof that you've failed.

- Trust that God has already equipped you for the journey.

2. Fear of Rejection (Relationships, Friendships, Social Settings)

Fear says: "What if they don't accept me? What if I get hurt?"

God says: "I have given you love to overcome fear."

- **Power:** Your worth is not based on others' opinions—it comes from who God says you are.

- **Love:** Love drives out fear. When we love freely, we focus on giving rather than fearing rejection. Romans 8:38-39 reminds us that nothing can separate us from God's love.

- **Sound Mind:** Instead of assuming the worst, approach relationships with wisdom and trust in God's plan.

Application:

- Stop overthinking people's reactions—be authentic and trust that the right people will value you.

- If someone rejects you, it's not a reflection of your worth—it may be God's way of redirecting you.

- Fill your mind with scriptures about your identity in Christ *(Ephesians 2:10, Psalm 139:14)*.

3. Fear of the Unknown (Future, Finances, Health, Life Changes)

Fear says: "I don't know what's going to happen. What if it all goes wrong?"

God says: "I have given you a sound mind to trust My plan."

- **Power:** You don't need to have all the answers—God does. Jeremiah 29:11 says He has a plan for your future.

- **Love:** When you trust in God's love, you know He won't let you down.

- **Sound Mind:** Instead of spiraling into anxiety, practice faith-based thinking: "If God has provided before, He will do it again."

Application:

- Instead of worrying, pray. Release your concerns to God *(Philippians 4:6-7)*.

- Take small steps toward your goals, trusting that God will guide each one.

- Remind yourself of past victories—if He did it before, He can do it again.

4. Fear of Stepping into Purpose (Calling, Ministry, Leadership)

Fear says: "I'm not qualified. What if I mess up?"

God says: "I have given you power to walk in your calling."

- **Power:** If God calls you, He equips you. Moses, Gideon, and Jeremiah, all doubted themselves, but God gave them strength.

- **Love:** Your purpose is bigger than you—it's about serving others. Love pushes you past fear and into action.

- **Sound Mind:** Trust that God will give you wisdom along the way. Proverbs 16:9 says, "A man's heart plans his way, but the Lord directs his steps."

Application:

- Take the first step, even if you feel unprepared. Growth happens in motion.

- Focus on obedience rather than perfection—God will handle the results.

- Surround yourself with people who encourage and sharpen you *(Proverbs 27:17)*.

Final Encouragement

Fear is a tool the enemy uses to paralyze and distract us from purpose. But 2 Timothy 1:7 is your weapon! Whenever fear creeps in, declare this verse over your life:

- **Power** to act
- **Love** that casts out fear
- A **sound mind** to think clearly and trust God

Challenge: Next time fear shows up, pause and ask, "What has God given me instead?" Then, step forward boldly!

NINE

FEAR HAS BECOME THE DRIVING FORCE OF THE MODERN WORLD

More than ever, people find themselves trapped in anxiety, uncertainty, and an overwhelming sense of instability. But why? The truth is, we've allowed ourselves to be conditioned by the noise around us rather than grounding ourselves in reality. We've become so consumed by fear that we've lost sight of what has always been true—life has never been certain. The illusion of control is just that: an illusion. Yet in today's world, we act as if uncertainty is something new, as if our struggles are unique to this time.

The reality is that nothing has ever been stable. Life has always been unpredictable. Jobs come and go, finances rise and fall, relationships shift, and circumstances change in an instant. The problem isn't the uncertainty itself—it's our resistance to it. Somewhere along the way, we convinced ourselves that stability was the norm—that we had control over the unseen and unknown. But that's never been the case. Instead of accepting uncertainty as a part of life, we've let fear shape our thoughts, actions, and even our beliefs.

Historically, people have endured wars, plagues, economic collapses, and personal hardship. Yet they survived, adapted, and moved forward. The same is true today. The fear we feel isn't because life is any more uncertain, it's because we're more aware of it. The constant flood of information, the pressure to predict and control outcomes, and the fear of the unknown have created a world driven by anxiety. But the truth is that we are no more in control today than we were in the past.

Biblically speaking, everything in this world is temporary. Ecclesiastes reminds us, "To everything, there is a season," pointing to the ever-changing nature of life. No matter how much we fight for stability, the reality stays the same, nothing here is permanent. The only certainty is that change is inevitable, and yet we continue to resist it, allowing fear to run our lives.

The key to overcoming fear is not to seek control—it's to embrace faith. Faith in God. Faith in yourself. Faith in the process. When we stop resisting and start accepting that uncertainty is a part of life, we free ourselves from fear's grip. Life was never meant to be controlled—only experienced.

And in that experience, we find strength, resilience, and peace.

The Cost of Staying Still

Why didn't I?" It's a question we hear far too often. Sometimes we just sit still and do nothing. We know we need change. We want better. We see the opportunities. But we remain stagnant.

We do nothing because of fear. We'd rather deal with the discomfort of being stuck and stagnant than face the unknown.

We convince ourselves that standing still is safer than moving forward. Fear of failure. Fear of rejection. Fear of not being enough. These invisible chains lock us in place. We say we'll act "when the time is right," but deep down, we know there's no such thing. The perfect moment is a lie we use to justify inaction.

Fear disguises itself as logic. It whispers excuses that sound reasonable: *I'm not ready yet. I need more information. What if I fail? What if I lose everything?* The more we listen, the more we convince ourselves that doing nothing is the right decision—even when we're miserable.

And so we sit. We wait. We watch opportunities go by. And we tell ourselves that if something is truly meant for us, it will come back around.

But life doesn't work that way.

Growth requires movement. Change takes action. Nothing transforms without effort. But still, we cling to the illusion that doing nothing is better than facing the unknown. And the unknown is terrifying because it doesn't come with guarantees. It requires trust, courage, and risk.

But here's the truth: the unknown also holds joy, success, breakthroughs, and transformation. You'll never experience any of that if you allow fear to paralyze you.

At some point, you have to ask: *Am I really living, or just existing?*

Existing is safe, but it's also stagnant. It's watching life happen instead of actively participating in it.

If you want more, if you truly desire growth, success, and fulfillment—you have to push past fear and step into the unknown, no matter how uncomfortable it may feel.

The choice is yours.

Stay stuck in fear.

Or move forward in faith.

TEN
UNCLOGGING YOUR ACCESS TO GOD

Many people live in fear without realizing that one of the biggest reasons they remain stuck in that fear is because their access to God is blocked. It's not that God isn't there, ready to guide and support them—it's that the connection has been clogged, like a pipe filled with debris. When a pipe is clogged, water can't flow freely. The same is true of your spiritual connection. Fear, worry, anxiety, and other negative emotions act like blockages, preventing you from experiencing the love, peace, and guidance that God is constantly offering.

Fear thrives in separation. When you feel distant from God, it becomes easier to believe you're alone in your struggles. The more you focus on fear, the more it takes root, making it harder to hear God's voice. Think of it like a clogged sink in your home—if you don't clear it, the blockage only gets worse over time. The same principle applies spiritually. The more fear, worry, and doubt you allow to accumulate, the harder it becomes to access the faith and clarity that would otherwise be flowing into your life.

Let's look at some of the most common spiritual blockages—starting with worry.

Worry is one of the most common blockages. It creates a cycle of overthinking and stress that clouds your mind and makes it difficult to trust God's plan. When you're consumed by worry, you're essentially saying your problems are bigger than God's power. But that's never the case. God is always greater, always present, and always willing to lead you through any storm. But you must be willing to let go of the mental clutter that keeps you disconnected from Him.

Anxiety is another major clog in the spiritual pipeline. It's rooted in fear of the unknown, fear of failure, or fear of loss. But Scripture reminds us, *"Do not be anxious about anything, but in every situation, by prayer and petition, with thanksgiving, present your requests to God"* (Philippians 4:6). Anxiety thrives when we try to control everything ourselves instead of surrendering our concerns to God. Trusting Him means believing that even when you don't see the solution, He is already working on your behalf.

Unresolved emotions like anger, resentment, and unforgiveness can also block your access to God. Holding onto these emotions is like allowing hair and grime to build up in a drain—it eventually stops the water from flowing altogether.

When you refuse to forgive, you cut yourself off from the healing and love that God wants to pour into your life. Jesus taught forgiveness not only for the benefit of others, but for your own spiritual well-being. Clearing these emotional blockages allows you to receive His love more fully.

I realized that unresolved emotions—especially the resentment I carried from my past experiences as a recording artist—were blocking my spiritual growth and keeping God from fully accessing my heart. It wasn't until I began studying biblical teachings on forgiveness that I understood what was holding me back. As I chose to release those negative emotions, I experienced a powerful shift. My perspective changed, and I began to see past challenges not as setbacks but as blessings. I've learned that forgiveness isn't only about extending grace to others, it's about freeing myself from the weight of emotional burdens. Now, I share my journey of transformation to empower others to find the same freedom I discovered.

So how do you unclog your spiritual connection?

First, acknowledge the blockages. Be honest with yourself about the fear, worry, or unresolved emotions that might be standing in your way.

Then, take intentional steps to clear them—through prayer, meditation, fasting, or seeking wise counsel.

Just as you would physically clean out a clogged pipe, you must spiritually clean out the thoughts and emotions that hinder your connection to God.

Finally, remember that God's love is always available to you. The flow has never stopped from His end—it's only been blocked by what you've allowed to build up in your heart and mind.

When you actively clear the blockages and open yourself up to His presence, you will experience a renewed sense of peace, courage, and divine guidance.

Fear loses its grip when love is fully present.

And God is love (1 John 4:8).

The more you align yourself with that truth, the freer you will become.

Where have you seen God's hand in your life this week?

What's one thing you did this week that you feel you could improve?

ELEVEN
LIVING IN THE PRESENT MOMENT

Fear thrives in the spaces where the past and future dominate our thoughts. When we fixate on past mistakes or anxiously anticipate what lies ahead, we create scenarios that don't exist in the present. These thoughts can paralyze us, making us hesitant to take action. The truth is that fear is often a projection of something that may never happen—or a memory of something that no longer has power over us. To overcome fear, we must shift our focus entirely to the moment we are in right now.

That shift starts with living in the present moment. It allows us to see reality for what it is, rather than what our fears make it out to be. The mind tends to exaggerate problems, weaving together worst-case scenarios that cloud our ability to act confidently.

But when we ground ourselves in the now, we remove the weight of imagined fears. Instead of fearing an uncertain future, we take steps based on what is real, right in front of us. The present moment is manageable—it's the only space where we truly have control.

One of the biggest obstacles to embracing the present is our attachment to the past. Past failures, disappointments, and pain linger in our minds and shape how we approach new opportunities. But the past is gone; it exists only in memory. Holding onto it only fuels hesitation and self-doubt. When we realize that the only moment that exists is now, we free ourselves from the burdens of yesterday. Our ability to act, decide, and move forward happens in this moment.

Similarly, worrying about the future keeps us trapped in fear. While planning and preparation are important, obsessing over what might go wrong limits our progress. The future is unpredictable. No amount of worrying can change that. Instead of fearing what hasn't happened, we must trust in our ability to face challenges as they come. When we stop letting imagined fears dictate our actions, we open ourselves to opportunities that we'd otherwise miss.

To live in the present, we must train our hearts and minds to be attentive to what God is doing right now. Fear often tries to pull us into the future or trap us in the past, but Scripture reminds us that God's grace is sufficient for *today*. As Jesus said, *"Therefore do not worry about tomorrow, for tomorrow will worry about itself. Each day has enough trouble of its own"* (Matthew 6:34, NIV).

When we shift our focus back to His presence, we find peace and strength. Prayer, worship, and meditating on God's Word anchor us in His truth and quiet the lies of fear. The more we lean into His presence daily, the more easily we can walk in faith, free from worry, and confident that He is in control.

For example: I've learned to put myself first, so that I can show up and be my better self. Now when I get up, I read a bible scripture, think about what I am grateful for, what concerns me. I fix my perspective. Sometimes I listen to motivational videos, walk and drink water.

Overcoming fear doesn't mean eliminating all discomfort or uncertainty—it's about learning to live in the moment, where fear has no power.

The mind will wander. It'll drag us into the past or push us into an imagined future. But if we discipline ourselves to stay in the now, to stay grounded, we see fear for what it is—a creation of the mind.

Reality isn't as frightening as we make it out to be.

In the end, freedom from fear lies in our ability to embrace the present moment. This is where life happens. This is where growth takes place. When we stop living in the past or the future and focus fully on what is real *right now*, we step into a life of clarity, strength, and purpose. Fear loses its power when we refuse to entertain it—and the only way to do that is by fully immersing ourselves in the present.

Life from a real standpoint

People often ask me, "How did you go from being an artist to doing all these other things? Weren't you afraid?" The truth is—yes. Fear was there. Doubt was there. But I learned that fear isn't the enemy. The real enemy is letting fear control your life.

We need to start looking at life from a real standpoint—not through the illusion of perfection or the highlight reels of social media, but through the lens of reality. And the reality is that nothing is perfect. We are imperfect beings—perfectly imperfect by design.

Once you embrace that, fear starts to lose its grip. Even at your lowest, even when you feel like you've failed, if you're still moving, you're still ahead of the person who never tried. Because you took action. You didn't allow those negative thoughts to hold you back.

Fear doesn't disappear—it evolves. It tests you. But the question is, will you let it stop you, or will you push forward anyway?

TWELVE

FEAR IS ONLY A FEELING

Fear is one of the most powerful emotions we experience. It can paralyze, control, and dictate the course of our lives if we let it. But at its core, fear is just that—an emotion. It is not a force that can physically stop you, nor is it an insurmountable wall. It's a response—a signal from your mind and body that something feels uncertain or threatening. The problem arises when we give fear more power than it deserves, allowing it to shape our decisions and limit our potential.

For many, fear feels so real that it becomes their reality. It whispers doubt into your mind, convincing you that failure is inevitable or that success is beyond your reach. It tells you that you're not good enough, smart enough, or capable enough. But here's the truth: fear is only a feeling, and feelings don't define you. They come and go, shifting like the wind. When you learn to recognize fear for what it is—just a temporary emotional state—you take away its ability to control your life.

The moment you separate yourself from fear, you begin to experience freedom. Think about the times when fear held you back. Was it fear of rejection that kept you from pursuing an opportunity? Was it fear of failure that stopped you from taking the first step?

Now, imagine if you had moved forward anyway, despite the fear. What would your life look like if fear no longer dictated your actions? The reality is that you don't have to imagine—you can live that way starting now.

To break free from fear, you must first change your relationship with it. Fear is not always a barrier—it can be a signal that you are stepping into something greater. It often shows up when you're on the verge of growth, right at the moment you're preparing to leave your comfort zone. That's why the most successful people don't wait for fear to disappear; they move forward in spite of it.

Take Tyler Perry as an example. He endured an abusive childhood and even experienced homelessness—circumstances that could have easily led to a lifetime of fear, rejection, and defeat. Yet, instead of allowing those setbacks to define him, he chose to confront fear head-on. That very fear became fuel, driving him to build a massive entertainment empire. Today, he stands as one of the most influential and inspirational voices in the industry, proof that fear doesn't have to hold you back, it can be the very thing that propels you forward.

One of the greatest lessons you can learn is that your feelings aren't facts. Just because you feel afraid doesn't mean you're in danger. Just because you feel uncertain doesn't mean you're unprepared. Feelings are fleeting—they don't have the power to define your destiny unless you let them. When you learn to acknowledge fear without giving it control, you become unstoppable.

Fear loses its power when you challenge it. The next time you feel afraid, ask yourself:

What am I really afraid of?

Is this fear based on truth or just emotion?

What would I do if fear weren't holding me back?

When you start questioning your fears instead of accepting them as reality, you take back your power. You shift from being a prisoner of fear to the master of your own life.

Living beyond your feelings means making choices based on your vision—not your emotions. It means refusing to let fear dictate your future. You have dreams, goals, and a purpose that's bigger than any passing emotion. The key is to recognize fear for what it is—just a feeling—and move forward anyway. When you do, you'll discover a life of limitless possibilities, a life no longer ruled by fear.

Fear Presents Itself In Habits That Feel Like Second Nature

Fear has a way of creeping into the smallest moments of our daily lives, often without us realizing it. It hides in how we navigate relationships, how we respond to uncertainty, and even in the simple act of decision-making.

A car ride with a significant other can turn into a moment of heightened anxiety when they question why you aren't paying attention. Their voice, filled with concern, breaks the silence as they watch the road with more fear than trust. A stop sign becomes a point of tension rather than a place to pause, as their nervous glances and fidgeting hands reveal a deeper unease. Fear manifests in ways that seem minor on the surface—but carry the weight of past experiences.

Sometimes, fear shows up in habits that feel like second nature. A person who double-checks the locks every night may not just be cautious; they may be reliving a time when security was taken from them. It's not just about avoiding an intruder—it's about the helplessness they once felt. These routines are a way of regaining control in a world that feels unpredictable.

Financial fear is another silent but powerful force. Some people avoid answering unknown numbers, dreading the possibility of a bill collector on the other end. Their stomach tightens at the thought of confrontation—even if no immediate consequence is coming. This fear often comes from a history of financial instability, where money became a source of shame, judgment, and emotional stress. It's not just about owing money; it's about the overwhelming sense of failure that can accompany financial struggles.

Fear can also be passed down through generations, shaping decisions, behaviors, and beliefs. A child who grows up watching their parents operate from a place of fear may internalize those same anxieties. If a mother constantly warns her children about the dangers of the outside world, they may grow up viewing everything as a potential threat. If a father is overly cautious with money, fearing financial ruin at every turn, his children may inherit a scarcity mindset, always afraid of losing what they have.

But the most dangerous thing about fear is how quietly it takes hold. It doesn't always announce itself. Sometimes it whispers, convincing you that your worries are justified, that playing it safe is the only option, and that taking risks means failure. It keeps you from trusting, moving forward, and embracing opportunities. But fear is not invincible. It can be questioned. It can be challenged. And most importantly, it can be overcome.

What if the thing you fear the most is actually the key to your breakthrough?

THIRTEEN

WHAT'S THE WORST THING THAT CAN HAPPEN?

Fear is something that holds many people back.

We often ask ourselves, *"What's the worst that can happen?"*—and then let that imagined worst-case scenario stop us from trying something new. But the truth is, the worst thing isn't failure. It's never trying at all.

Life moves forward whether we're ready or not, and fear only keeps us stuck. We spend so much time worrying about things we think we can control, but the biggest changes in life are usually the ones we never see coming.

Fear tricks us into believing we have control over what happens.

We plan. We worry. We hesitate. And we think these things will help us avoid failure. But no matter how much we try to predict the future, life has a way of surprising us. And the things we fear—like rejection or embarrassment—are often not as bad as we imagined.

Meanwhile, the things we never feared—unexpected events, or sudden changes, such as losing a job, or the unexpected loss of a loved one—are the ones that truly change our lives the most.

So why do we give fear so much of our time?

When something unexpected happens, we don't have time to be afraid—we just react. And most of the time, we handle it better than we thought we would.

Fear doesn't protect us. It paralyzes us.

If we trusted ourselves more, we'd see that we can handle whatever comes our way, whether we expect it or not.

If we really believed that, we'd live more freely. We wouldn't let fear stop us from taking risks. We'd try new things. Instead of worrying about failure, we would focus on the possibilities.

Life is full of unknowns. No one can predict what's ahead. But if we keep letting fear make our decisions, we'll miss out on the best experiences in life.

Fear will always be there. But we don't have to listen to it.

We get to choose. Will we let fear control us, or will we step forward anyway?

The unknown is scary—but it's also full of opportunities.

Some of the best things in life happen when we stop letting fear hold us back and take a chance on the unknown.

FOURTEEN

FEAR OF HOW OTHERS PERCEIVE YOU

People often fear failure—but what scares them even more is how others will see them if they fail. We live in a world where people try to present themselves as perfect, especially on social media. Everyone wants to look like they have everything under control, as if their life is smooth and without problems. But the truth is that no one is perfect. Everyone struggles. Sometimes the fear of looking weak or vulnerable can be even greater than the fear of failing itself.

The fear of being judged can hold us back from taking risks. Instead of focusing on personal growth, we worry about how we'll look to others if we stumble. This mindset can prevent us from reaching our full potential. When we care too much about our public image, we often choose comfort over opportunity—and miss out on chances to learn and grow.

Ironically, vulnerability is a sign of strength. When someone is open about their struggles and failures, it shows courage and honesty. Others respect and can relate to those willing to share their challenges. No one connects with perfection because it isn't real. But people are inspired by those who continue pushing forward despite difficulties and setbacks.

The pressure to appear perfect is not only unrealistic, it's unhealthy. It can cause stress, anxiety, and even depression. Constantly pretending to be someone you are not is exhausting. Instead of chasing an image of perfection, it's better to embrace authenticity. Being open about both successes and struggles builds deeper connections and brings more happiness in life.

In the end, we can't let the fear of looking imperfect control us. Everyone experiences failure— it's a natural part of growth. True confidence comes from accepting ourselves— flaws and all. When we stop worrying so much about how others see us, we can start to truly live.

When you are not living your true, authentic life, fear tends to take the lead. But those who reconnect with their authentic selves often find they are less fearful in every area of life. They have a clear understanding of their boundaries, their challenges, and what makes them uncomfortable—and they have the courage to be honest about it.

Many people, however, choose to hide these truths. Out of fear, they walk away from opportunities rather than admitting when something feels out of their element or beyond their current capacity. Yet, if they would simply acknowledge it, they would create space for others to step in, offer support, and meet them exactly where they are.

FIFTEEN
THE GLASSES
WE WEAR

Have you ever thought about the glasses we all wear?

Each of us walks through life wearing invisible glasses—lenses shaped by our experiences, traumas, victories, and beliefs. These glasses determine how we see the world. They filter every moment, every relationship, every opportunity.

As I took my early morning walk today, I reflected on this. I thought about how some of us are wearing shattered glasses—cracked by pain, betrayal, fear, and disappointment. These broken lenses distort reality and rob us of clarity. They keep us stuck in a cycle of fear because what we see is shaped by what we've been through.

But here's the beautiful truth: we have the power to change our glasses.

We can replace the broken lenses. We can choose to see life differently—to see it through hope, purpose, and love. The hard part isn't putting on new glasses, it's taking off the old ones.

Especially when we've worn them for so long, they start to feel normal. Comfortable, even. We stop noticing the cracks.

Sometimes we know it's time. Deep down, we feel it. But we resist—afraid of what we'll see without the old lenses. Still, there comes a moment—an awakening—when we must admit the truth: we're seeing life through outdated eyes. And it's time for a new pair.

It's a new day.

Despite the challenges you've faced . . . despite the obstacles that tried to break you . . . it's a new day. And you have the power to shift. To take back control. To move beyond fear. To see life differently and rise again. The power is within you. But you don't have to do it alone.

Sometimes taking the glasses off means sitting down with someone who can help you see yourself clearly—a therapist, a mentor, a friend who truly listens. It means confronting the pain you've buried. Getting honest about the fear that's been quietly driving your decisions.

Taking the glasses off requires courage—but also compassion. You have to be gentle with yourself. You have to give yourself permission to heal. That might look like journaling through your truth. It might look like prayer, meditation, therapy, or simply saying, "I need help."

You don't take them off all at once. Sometimes it's one crack at a time being healed. One conversation. One realization. One deep breath when anxiety rises. One decision to try again.

Letting go of the broken lenses doesn't mean pretending your past didn't happen. It means refusing to let it define your future.

You deserve new vision. You deserve to see yourself as whole again—to see life as full of possibility.

It's your time. Your healing. Your new beginning.

Take the glasses off—and see.

Being Honest with Yourself

Being honest with yourself is one of the most powerful things you can do.

Many times, we take on too much. We say yes to things when we should say no. We involve ourselves in situations that aren't ours to carry. And this leads to stress, confusion, and fear.

Sometimes we try to live a life that isn't really ours. We buy things we can't afford. We try to keep up with others instead of focusing on what's best for us. Every month, we stress about how we'll pay for things we should never have signed up for in the first place. The pressure builds—and fear sets in.

The truth is that many of us don't want to admit where we are in life. We don't want to face the fact that we're struggling. So we hide behind appearances. But the longer we avoid it, the harder it becomes to move forward.

Being honest about your situation is the first step toward change.

It's okay to say, "I can't handle this right now." It's okay to step back and focus on yourself. Life has seasons—and some seasons are meant for rest and rebuilding, not for adding more.

When we take on more than we can handle, we burn out mentally, emotionally, and financially.

We live in a world that pushes us to keep going, to keep doing more. But we need to ask ourselves: Am I in a position to add more to my life right now? Or am I just trying to prove something to other people?

Check in with yourself.

Are you taking care of your health? Sleeping enough? Eating well? Are your relationships healthy—or are you letting toxic ones drain you?

Are you being honest about how we truly feel?

People-pleasing can become a trap. When you constantly give to others but forget yourself, you end up empty. You start living for everyone else, and that creates more stress and fear. You worry about what people will think if you say no.

Being honest is freeing. When you stop pretending and start living in your truth, you gain peace. You may lose approval—or even some relationships—but you will gain something greater: your peace, your sanity, your freedom.

Today, many people are silently struggling. They've lost jobs. They're stuck with bills they can't pay. They have homes they can't afford to keep. But instead of asking for help or downsizing, they suffer in silence, fearing judgment.

At the end of the day, being honest with yourself is the only way to grow. It's how you make better choices. It's how you protect your peace. It's how you take control of your life.

Honesty might be hard at first—but it will set you free.

Check your lenses—what are they showing you today?

SIXTEEN

THE DIGITAL AGE
AND US

In today's world, cell phones have become almost an extension of ourselves. We carry them everywhere—a constant source of news, social media updates, and entertainment. This chapter explores how our dependency on devices affects our minds and lives.

Not long ago, most people got their news from just a few sources, like the local newspaper or the evening news. Today, however, we're flooded with headlines from hundreds of news outlets, blogs, and social media accounts. This shift in the way we get information has changed how we learn about the world around us.

Every time we pick up our phones, we're exposed to stories of violence, disasters, and political turmoil. Over time, this constant exposure to negative news can leave us feeling anxious, overwhelmed, and fearful. Too much bad news can take a toll on our mental health, leading to stress and even depression.

Social media platforms were designed to keep us connected—but they also bombard us with opinions and sensational content. Have you ever found yourself reaching for your phone without even thinking? Our brains are wired to seek rewards. Notifications and likes can become addictive.

Spending too much time on our phone, especially absorbing negative news, can harm our well-being and affect our relationships. It can cause anxiety, stress, and sleep disturbances.

So what happens when you put your phone down?

Disconnecting from digital devices, even for a short time, can reduce anxiety and help us refocus on what matters most in life. Mindfulness, the practice of paying attention to the present moment without judgment—can help us manage the constant flow of information.

Technology isn't all bad. It brings convenience, connection, and access to endless information. But balance is key. Set limits on screen time and choose quality over quantity.

By choosing when to engage and when to disconnect, we can regain control over our lives.

Action Steps:

1. Put Your Phone Down

    Start by setting aside a specific time each day when you intentionally put your phone down. Use that time to relax, connect with friends, or enjoy a hobby. This simple act of disconnecting can help you reclaim your focus and reduce the constant bombardment of information.

2. Unfollow Unnecessary Feeds

    Review the blogs and social media accounts you follow. Identify those that frequently share negative or overwhelming content and consider unfollowing or muting them. This can help reduce mental clutter and decrease anxiety.

3. Streamline Your News Sources

    Instead of jumping between multiple news outlets that often repeat the same stories, choose one reputable source with balanced coverage. It's enough to stay informed without feeling overloaded.

We are in a state of mental overload, social media, endless streaming, we are on high alert every day. It has reduced our attention span.

By taking these practical steps, putting your phone down, unfollowing unnecessary feeds, and streamlining your news sources, you create a healthier relationship with technology.

Remember, the goal isn't to disconnect completely but to reclaim your peace of mind and make space for what matters most.

These actionable steps will help reduce digital overload and lead to a more mindful, balanced life—even in our increasingly connected world.

SEVENTEEN

THE SOLUTION: THE MOMENT YOU'VE BEEN WAITING FOR

I've given you a lot of conversation, insight, and under-standing—and some help with fear. But I believe this is the real solution . . . the key to navigating uncertainty and fear of the unknown.

And I know that after reading this book, you might be thinking, "Wait a minute. I'm at the end of the book and you're just now giving me the solution?"

Maybe you thought the solution would be a twenty-page answer to a single question. But just remember this:

Fear is simply not real. It's a response. It's how you perceive what's in front of you based on your life experiences—

trauma, environment, upbringing, family, and everything else you were exposed to from the moment you entered this world. From the moment you were born, you were shaped by the world around you.

All of these things have played a part in how you see reality and which challenges bring you the most fear.

But I want you to never forget this:

The way you took on those obstacles and developed a fearful outlook on life is the same way you can free yourself from those obstacles and change that outlook.

So to sum it up, if you want to get rid of fear, you must live in reverse. And that means rewinding yourself.

So take a pen and pad, and start writing:

- Write the moments you remember.
- Write the experiences you had growing up.
- Write the moments when you felt hopeless, unsafe, or unprotected as a child.

As you remember those moments, I want you to repeat after me:

My past doesn't define my future.

However, my future is stagnated by my past.

The way I see the world and the things around me should no longer affect me the way they have.

I must rewire myself and delete those old, stored memories by seeking professional help with a licensed therapist.

But more importantly, I must understand that we live only in the present moment.

There is nothing else outside of right now.

Everything else is just a thought.

We must learn to live in the moment. We must take every moment seriously and use the time we have to truly work on ourselves.

And at the end of the day—what is there to be afraid of?

Yes, we all have fears. I have fears. But fear is just false evidence—evidence we've collected from our past experiences. And most of that evidence? It came from people who refused to do the work themselves—and it trickled down to us.

Now, let's get out there and do the work. Let's face this thing we call fear.

And one last thing—this isn't an overnight journey. I'm still working on it myself. But at least now I know that there's hope. There's an opportunity to change how we see life—our obstacles, our challenges, our ups and downs, the things that bother us, the uncertainty of it all.

There's an opportunity to shift our perspective.

Just remember that none of the things we worry about—if they're material—can go with us anyway. Some of the opportunities we lost, some of the jobs we didn't get, might have actually been blessings in disguise.

Yes, uncertainty is scary, especially for those of us with families and children. But please, hear me loud and clear:

Things can change.

Things will change.

But they won't change in the way you expect them to.

Once you start doing the work, your entire approach to life will change. And the people around you? They'll benefit too. You'll realize something powerful: we have no control over anything. Everything is uncertain. So why carry all this stress and fear? Why take on the weight of the world, only to realize that control was never in our hands to begin with?

Let it all go.

The Solution: How to Stay True to Yourself

First, you have to understand this:

You are enough just being you.

Your worth is not based on your job, your success, your relationship, or what people think about you.

Here's what you can start doing:

1. **Spend Time Getting to Know Yourself Again**

    Take time to figure out who you are without the titles, money, relationship, or fame.

    Ask yourself:

    *   What makes me happy?
    *   What makes me laugh?
    *   What do I love doing even if no one claps for me?

    Write it down if you have to. You need to know who you are when the lights are off and no one is watching.

2. Practice Saying "No"

You don't have to say yes to everything and everyone. Saying no protects your peace. If something doesn't feel right to you, it's okay to say no—even if people get mad.

Remember: if saying yes hurts you, it's the wrong yes.

3. Stop Chasing Validation

You don't need everyone to like you.

If the whole world claps for you, but you don't clap for yourself, you'll never be happy.

Start by asking:

- Do I like me?
- Am I proud of who I am?

Your opinion of yourself matters more than anyone else's.

4. Learn to Let Go

If people walk away because you're being your true self, let them go.

The right people will love you for who you really are.

Don't hold onto people who only like the "performance" version of you.

5. Stay Connected to What You Love

Don't let success or failure change your heart.

Keep doing the things you love—even if no one's paying you, even if no one's watching.

This keeps you grounded and close to your real self.

6. Be Patient With Yourself

Healing and growing takes time.

You may slip up. You may have days where you feel lost again. That's okay.

Just don't give up.

Keep choosing yourself, every day.

In simple words:

You don't have to perform.

You don't have to shrink.

You don't have to fake it.

You just have to be real—and protect that realness like your life depends on it. Because it does.

EIGHTEEN
HAPPINESS ON THE OTHER SIDE OF FEAR

No matter how long the journey, how hard the work, or how many obstacles stand in your way— pushing through will always be worth it. On the other side of fear, possibilities are endless, and growth has no limits.

When you break through that barrier—when you shatter that glass—you'll realize that the only thing that was holding you back was your willingness to face your fears.

Not just to confront them, but to understand them. To see that fear is nothing more than an emotion. One that built a stronghold in your life for too long.

But now . . .

You're free. You've done the work. You've stepped into your power.

And it's time to enjoy everything you've fought for.

It's been a long, tough journey—but I have to say I'm proud of you.

You've overcome your fears.

You've chosen yourself.

Thank you for reading this book.

But more importantly—thank you for believing in yourself enough to do the work. Your future is limitless.

Enjoy every moment.

You're not alone. You've got this.

Affirmations are powerful tools that shape the way we think, feel, and act. In a world filled with uncertainty, negativity, and constant noise, it's easy to let fear or doubt take the lead. But by speaking life over ourselves daily, we begin to reframe our mindset and align with truth, peace, and strength.

To get the most out of affirmations, consistency is key. Set aside a few quiet moments each day—morning, evening, or whenever you need a reset—to speak them aloud. Write them in a journal, place them on sticky notes around your home or workspace, or even record yourself saying them and listen back. What matters most is repetition and belief. The more you affirm truth, the more it becomes part of you.

As you read through the affirmations in this chapter, choose the ones that resonate most deeply. Make them personal, adapt them to your situation, and return to them often. Over time, these words will not just be sentences you repeat, but a new way of living—grounded in hope, courage, and faith.

1. Self-Worth & Confidence
(Loving yourself, being proud of who you are)

- I am enough.
- I am worthy just as I am.
- I deserve love for being me.
- My voice matters.
- I trust myself.
- I am not my past.
- I am valuable.
- I am proud of who I am.
- I am beautiful inside and out.
- I am not competing with anyone.
- I deserve respect in every space I enter.
- I am a magnet to blessings.
- I am confident in who I am.
- I am more than enough.
- I am proud to be exactly who I am.

2. Healing & Forgiveness
(Letting go of pain and moving forward)

- I forgive myself for my past mistakes.
- I release what no longer serves me.
- I trust my ability to heal.
- I am healing from things I don't even talk about.
- I allow myself to rest.
- I honor my healing journey.
- I release shame.

- I release guilt.
- I forgive myself for settling in the past.
- I forgive myself for not knowing better before.
- I am breaking old cycles.
- I trust the lessons life brings me.
- I don't have to rush my healing.
- I am letting go of old versions of me.
- I trust myself more every day.

3. Authenticity & Living Free
(Being your real self, without fear)

- I am brave enough to be real.
- I don't have to prove anything to anyone.
- It's okay to say no.
- I choose authenticity.
- I speak my truth.
- I live in my truth.
- I refuse to hide my greatness.
- I refuse to settle for less.
- I allow myself to be fully seen.
- I walk in my truth boldly.
- I choose myself and I'm proud of it.
- I give myself permission to be proud.
- I honor myself by showing up as ME.

4. Setting Boundaries & Protecting Peace
(Saying no, guarding energy)

- I protect my peace.
- I protect my energy.
- I honor my boundaries.
- I am no longer available for fake love.
- I am no longer available for fake friendships.
- I deserve to be treated right.
- I walk away from anything that disrespects me.
- I don't have to carry other people's opinions.
- I know when to walk away.
- I say no without guilt.
- I move at my own pace.
- I keep my peace no matter what.
- I have the right to say no.

5. Faith, Growth, and Moving Forward
(Trusting the process, not quitting)

- I trust the timing of my life.
- I believe better days are ahead.
- I choose faith over fear.
- I am becoming the best version of me.
- I trust the path I'm walking.
- I am right where I'm supposed to be.
- I trust myself to get there.
- I celebrate every small victory.
- I am becoming someone my future will thank.

- I trust that what's meant for me will find me.
- I welcome new beginnings.
- I deserve real happiness.
- I rise every time I fall.
- I have the heart to keep believing.
- I have the strength to rebuild.

100 AFFIRMATIONS TO HELP YOU REMAIN YOUR TRUE SELF

1. I am enough.

2. I am worthy just as I am.

3. I choose myself every day.

4. I don't have to prove anything to anyone.

5. I am proud of who I am.

6. I deserve love for being me.

7. I trust myself.

8. I believe in myself.

9. My voice matters.

10. I am stronger than my fears.

11. I honor my true feelings.

12. I am not here to please everyone.

13. It's okay to say no.

14. I respect my own boundaries.

15. My opinion counts.

16. I am more than my job.

17. I am more than my mistakes.

18. I am growing every day.

19. I am allowed to change.

20. I choose peace over pressure.

21. I deserve to be happy.

22. I don't need outside approval to feel good inside.

23. I listen to my heart.

24. I am proud of my journey.

25. I am proud of my scars.

26. I am enough without a title.

27. I am brave enough to be real.

28. I forgive myself for past mistakes.

29. I give myself permission to be happy.

30. I trust my own path.

31. I am not my past.

32. I am not my failures.

33. I am not my fears.

34. I am bigger than my problems.

35. I am growing into my best self.

36. I deserve real love.

37. I attract real connections.

38. I release what no longer serves me.

39. I accept myself fully.

40. I am proud of my progress.

41. I don't have to chase love.

42. I don't have to earn acceptance.

43. I am valuable.

44. I am powerful.

45. I am a light in this world.

46. I allow myself to rest.

47. I am learning and growing every day.

48. I give myself grace.

49. I choose joy.

50. I choose authenticity.

51. I let go of fear.

52. I let go of doubt.

53. I let go of guilt.

54. I am free to be myself.

55. I shine my true light.

56. I am at peace with who I am.

57. I respect my own journey.

58. I celebrate my wins.

59. I learn from my losses.

60. I trust the timing of my life.

61. I am right where I'm supposed to be.

62. I release what weighs me down.

63. I protect my energy.

64. I protect my peace.

65. I listen to my soul.

66. I deserve happiness without pain.

67. I am not too much.

68. I am not too little.

69. I am just right.

70. I am bold.

71. I am fearless.

72. I am courageous.

73. I take up space.

74. I deserve to be seen.

75. I deserve to be heard.

76. I honor my inner child.

77. I speak my truth.

78. I live in my truth.

79. I am grounded.

80. I am confident.

81. I do not need permission to be myself.

82. I do not shrink for others.

83. I choose me.

84. I love myself unconditionally.

85. I am loyal to my dreams.

86. I believe better days are ahead.

87. I walk in purpose.

88. I walk in power.

89. I walk in peace.

90. I walk in love.

91. I deserve to rest.

92. I deserve to grow.

93. I deserve to heal.

94. I welcome good things.

95. I welcome new beginnings.

96. I attract positive energy.

97. I deserve freedom.

98. I am grateful for my journey.

99. I am grateful for my strength.

100. I am grateful for my life.